CW00518243

Seaside Entrepreneurs

Carol Edwards

ISBN 978-0-9562201-1-0

Published by Carol Edwards
2010

Sources

Southend Museum
Essex Record Office
Southend Library/Local Studies Section
Francis Frith Collection
The Jaquest Family
Frank Dutton
David Allen
Carol Mulrony
Media Department Southend-on-Sea
Absalom Bathing Machines courtesy of Francis Frith Collection

Acknowledgements

My sincere thanks to Wendy Clarke, for all her assistance over many months, in obtaining photographs, information and arranging interviews with her extended Jaquest family.

My thanks to my husband Barry for his technical support

Marion Hough for encouraging me to continue writing

And Chris for helping me compile this book and designing the cover.

Contents

The Absaloms—Wandsworth—Southend-on-Sea 1700s—1990s

The Jaquests—Marylebone—Southend-on-Sea 1854—Present Day

The Absaloms

Wandsworth — Southend-on-Sea

1700s — 1990s

Introduction

Henry Absalom, a fisherman (1827 – 1904) and John Jaquest bricklayer (1854 – 1939) had nothing in common and were not destined to meet but both men would be given the chance to make changes to their lives, which would improve their standard of living by the various businesses with which they would become involved. To understand how it all came about we must look at the social changes and history of visiting the seaside which presented these two men with the opportunity of transforming their working lives.

In the early 1700s the area was known as the South End of Prittlewell, quite poor and undeveloped, it was really nothing more than a small fishing village with cottages scattered along the shore, mainly inhabited by fishermen and labourers. It was to this area that the Absaloms would move many years later, becoming mariners and fisherman. During the reign of George III, who came to the throne in 1760, the number of visitors to South End began to increase, but at this point it was only the well to do and upper classes who could afford to travel. Many came down from London by stagecoach, which took several hours over bumpy unmade roads, alternatively they took one of the many passenger sailing ships, operating on the Thames during that period. These ships would later be replaced by steamers which could make the journey much faster than those with sails. Although the journey itself was more relaxing, offering the traveller the time to enjoy the sea air and converse with their fellow passengers, the disadvantage became obvious when they reached the resort and found the tide to be out.

1

Formerly Hope Hotel

Unfortunately there would always be a small gulley of water to cross and this was achieved by using small rowing boats which would deposit their charges onto the hard shingle, from where they would be expected to walk to the shore. To this short walk would often result in mud on the bottom of the gentlemen's trousers and along the hems of the ladies sweeping skirts. By 1830 a pier had been built, some 1, 500 feet in length, but at low tide it was still not long enough for the ships to dock along side its wooden structure.

When the new fashion for taking the waters was adopted by royalty – Princesses Caroline and Charlotte – it was a foregone conclusion that society would soon follow suit and be venturing into the water. For people to come and indulge in this new fad, accommodation was required and the first inn to be built along Lower South End was The Ship. Also for the benefit of the visitor was the Caroline Baths built at the far end of Lower South End, on a site occupied today (2010) by the Sea Life Centre. The baths offered hot and cold water to the discerning bather. With propriety demanding that ladies should not be seen in their swimming costumes, the arrival in 1750 of bathing machines was perfect to protect their modesty. Although the type of costumes worn in the 18th century covered the wearer from top to toe leaving no part of the body exposed.

Royal Terrace overlooking the shrubbery

The moneyed classes continued to dominate Southend-on-Sea for many years, their numbers increasing to such a degree that more hotels and accommodation were built to house them during their stay. Entertainment was also provided at the local theatre with plays or musical evenings. The class of visitor would remain unchanged until around the middle of the 1800s when social changes began to allow the working classes to enjoy some of the pleasures previously enjoyed only by the rich. It would be the arrival of steam trains and bank holidays, introduced by Sir John Lubbock, that would change the whole concept of a day at the seaside for all. The LTS – The London Tilbury and Southend Railway, finally reached the end of the line out of Fenchurch Street in 1856. The journey was quick in comparison to road and sea travel and was far more reasonably priced. This meant that people on lower incomes could afford to travel on this new mode of transport and cover greater distances. But it was in 1871 when parliament passed the act introduced by Lubbock, that the working classes could enjoy weekends away by the seaside. This major development brought sweeping changes around the country and was instrumental in changing the face not only of Southend but many other seaside destinations as well.

As the trippers (as they became known) came in their thousands, all looking to be fed, entertained and like their so called betters, take to the waters, lodging houses cafes and public houses began springing up all along the road which was opposite the beach. Called Marine Parade it had once been an area of grand private houses, where families such as the Vandervoords had lived. They were a wealthy family who owned a large fleet of barges used to ship grain and other products around the country. Their once beautiful homes were now converted to serve the new seaside trade. This area was still known as Lower South End with upper South End firmly established at the top of Pier Hill, with the Royal Hotel and Royal Terrace overlooking the shrubbery and Thames. This was where the rich and famous would stay. A publication of the day described the two areas as; "Upon the wooden hill stands new Southend, or the upper town. A steep road leads down to old Southend"

For those staying in their fancy hotels or lodgings at the top of the hill, there was no desire to mix with what they considered to be the rowdy working classes at the bottom of the hill. So the more sophisticated visitor to the town would take the air, listen to concerts enter the water and partake of food along Western Esplanade. For the rest the Derbyshire guide of the day described what was on offer in lower Southend: "The Marine Parade does a roaring trade in teas and Shrimps as big as lobsters. The ice cream, cockles and oysters are second to none". At one time Southend was renowned for its oysters. Increasing numbers of visitors to the town and the resulting extra sewerage would eventually destroy the oyster beds.

Providing for the needs of these working class trippers, offered the locals so many opportunities to earn extra money. Among them was Henry Absalom who began renting out bathing machines, before taking on many other seaside ventures between 1870 – 1904. John Jaquest's time came later between 1908 – 1939 when with his family they played their part in serving the holidaymaker through their shops and restaurants on Eastern Esplanade near to the Kursaal.

The story of the Absaloms and Jaquests offers an insight into how the arrival of steam trains, better working conditions for the lower classes and new ways to spend their limited free time, gave these two quite ordinary men the opportunity to become seaside entrepreneurs.

4

Surname Absalom
Origins and Spellings

The surname Absalom is said to have been derived from the Hebrew "Avshalom" meaning peace. The name however is not just associated with the Jewish community as the name is quite common across the spectrum. There are many variant forms of spelling the name, Absalom, Absolon, Abselom Absolom, and Aspenlon all of which could be found in England in medieval times. The most common and enduring spelling appears to be Absolon. One of the earliest records, details a Thomas Absolon on the "Curia Regis Rolls Of Oxfordshire" in 1208. As the population grew the surname became quite common in Berkshire, in areas such as North Morton, Bray and Cholsey. The surname, with different spellings, could also be found in small numbers in Gillingham in Kent and Bruton in Somerset around the same period. As we approach the 1600s although there are still Absaloms living in Berkshire, we start to see the name becoming quite prolific in Wales. In particular around, Mynyddislwn in Monmouth, Merthyr Tydfil in Glamorgon and Haverfordwest in Pembroke. By the 1800s in keeping with the times, when people deserted the countryside for the towns and cities, the Absaloms being no different headed to London, although they were not the first to arrive in the city as William Absalom is shown to be residing in Cripplegate as early as 1571. The numbers of Absaloms or Absolons increased steadily in London over the centuries.

Exploring Henry Absalom's family before they moved to the South End of Prittlewell, we find that the original spelling for John Absalom and his children was in fact, Absolon. Within a few years the spelling was changed to Absalom. This was unlikely to have been of their own making, more likely to have come about due to the fact that many could not read or write and therefore scribes wrote names down as they saw fit.

When the Wandsworth Absaloms arrived in Prittlewell the early 1800s they were the only family in the area with that surname. Although their number at first increased, as the children married and had their own families, with infant mortality and early deaths, for the adults, quite common, the Absaloms decreased in size as they approached 1900, after which the name disappeared altogether in Southend-on-Sea by the late 1990s.

The Path to Change and Prosperity
Fisherman to Businessman

The path to change and prosperity, that saw lower South End grow from a fishing hamlet in the 1700's, to a thriving seaside destination, did not occur overnight. As its popularity slowly grew over the years and the number of visitors wanting to "take the waters" increased, so did the opportunities for those fisherman living in lower South end, to supplement their income. First came bathing machines on the beach and indoor warm water baths in the hotels. Not everyone was convinced that swimming in the Thames, was beneficial to the individuals health. A report in a Gentleman's magazine in 1792 reported that a sea-bathing infirmary was to be built on a parcel of land, donated by Daniel Scratton. The building was intended to house thirty beds to care for those affected by having taken a dip or swim in the sea water. Needless to say the infirmary never materialised. It is somewhat ironic however that the danger lay not in the sea but the warm water baths. Before the days of health and safety one of these establishments was subject to a report in 1870 in the local paper the Southend Standard :

> The bath for gentlemen only was very cramped
> and it was not uncommon for bathers to die
> in the changing room and their bodies not
> be found until the next day.

With the arrival in 1856 of the railway , travelling by train from London direct into Southend was not only faster than previous modes of transport , but cheaper as well. When three public holidays a year were introduced, Easter Monday, Whit Monday and August Bank Holiday, the masses poured into the town all looking for a good day out. The locals rose to the challenge and beer houses, cafes and shops, sprang up along the busy Parade opposite the Thames. The local fishermen also advertised trips from the beach, in their rowing and sailing boats, offering to take the individual away from the hustle and bustle of the crowded promenade, to the relative peace and quiet on the water. For two men, both members of local fishing families, Henry Absalom and Thomas Ingram would find their lives transformed by this new fad for the seaside. Although Thomas set the path that Henry would follow I feel that as this book is devoted more to the Absaloms that is where I should begin.....

Charles Absalom was a River Police Officer 1890—1899

Colchester Police Officers working on the River Colne 1800s, protecting the oyster beds

Photographs by courtesy of Essex Police Museum

The Absaloms

The family originated from Wandsworth and their roots can be traced back in that area, to 1704. James Absalom was born there in 1758 and later married an Ann Wragg, with whom he had nine children. Six daughters and three sons. As it is always easier to trace a family's history through the male line, I will follow their son's James (1791), Henry (1795) and Robert (1806) but I will not neglect a wife or two or daughters, who married and still have descendants living in the area today (2010). I do not however intend to chart the whole extended family but merely to show how some of its members, adapted and used the changing social circumstances that surrounded them to improve their standard of living. Not all took up new seaside trades, but remained fisherman but this in itself, meant they were able to provide the many and varied eating places with the fish needed to feed the visitor.

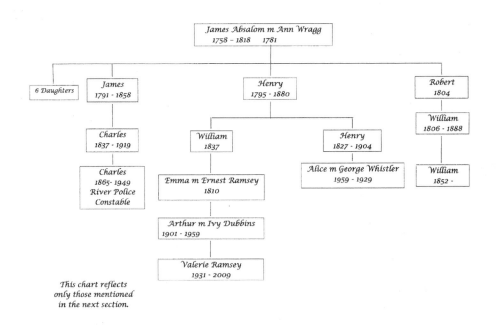

This chart reflects only those mentioned in the next section.

The family are first recorded on settlement papers in 1813 as renting two cottages in Prittlewell, from a Richard Mathews at 4s per week. Later James (1758) is shown to be on the parish, meaning that through either ill health or lack of work had no income. His death came in 1818 by which time his sons were adults and caring for themselves. By 1841 James and Robert are married and living with their families just a few doors from one another in Wellington Place, close to the shore and opposite where many years later the Kursaal would be built. Both men give their occupations as watermen. For Robert and his son's, they continued the tradition through three generations. For James(1758) his grandson Charles born in 1865, would deviate for a few years during his working life as a fisherman, when in 1890 he changed course completely when he joined Colchester Borough Police. Soon after, The Colne River Fishery Committee, asked for a police presence on the river to protect their oyster beds and a sergeant and three constables were thus employed. Charles was a natural choice for one of the constables to patrol the river. He remained in the force until 1899 when he returned to Southend, where he was able to buy his own

boat, this came at a time when the town's visitors were reaching their peak and he would have been able to offer trips on the water in the summer months and return to fishing in the winter.

Life for William born in 1837, when his first wife died, leaving him with three daughters to raise, meant for a time he had to give up fishing to work as a fish salesman from his home on Marine Parade. Later through one of his daughters, Emma (1870) he would move into the building trade with his son-in-law Ernest Ramsey who married Emma in 1888. By profession Ernest was a carpenter and joiner, later he would be listed as a builder.

Valerie as a child
Grand daughter of
William Absalom

Valerie Dutton nee
Ramsey

Together they submitted plans to Southend Board of Health to build three cottages in Sutton Street, Southend in 1899. William was to live in number 39, with his second wife and four children. The property next to his was rented out to a Thomas Thipthorpe a carpenter. William's daughter Emma and her family lived at number 43. Through Emma and Ernest Ramsey today we still have some of their descendants living in the town. Peter Ramsey and Valerie Dutton nee Ramsey until she passed away in 2009. Through her son Frank who now lives in Australia I learnt a little of the family's continuing association with Southend-on-Sea to the present day. Another Absalom daughter, Alice (1858) married George Whistler, today some of their direct descendants are still living in Southchurch.

When William Absalom (1852) was away from home on the fishing boats, his wife Marion ran a lodging house, which could not have been easy as she had five young children to care for during this period in the 1890s. With their house in Hartington Road, quite near the seafront and being somewhat larger than the average cottage in the area, it was ideally suited to offer rooms for those wishing to stay a night or two in the town. In the heart of lower South End, during the same period, Harry Absalom was a beer house keeper right on the main strip – Marine Parade. During the summer months and especially bank holidays business would have been brisk, as thousands of people came to the town to enjoy one of their few holidays. Harry would later work for his father Henry (1827) managing his bathing machines.

For Henry (1795) the last of the three sons of James and Ann Absalom life would not be complicated by changing profession or supplementing his income with other occupations, he remained a fisherman his whole working life. It would be left to his son born in 1827 to break the mould and became a seaside entrepreneur. Henry lived to a ripe old age dying in 1880, enough time to witness his eldest son's success as a businessman.

With a greater number of daughters having being born to the Absaloms, there has to be many people today, in and around the town related to this family who lived through a time of great change on the seafront of both upper and lower Southend.

The Ingrams

My reason for adding this section on the Ingram family is that where they went Henry Absalom (1827) was to follow.

The shrubbery 2010

Among the first of many fishermen living in lower Southend to see the potential of supplementing their income, by providing amenities for the towns new seaside visitors, was one Thomas Ingram, born in 1781. With indoor warm baths already established in the town (the Caroline Baths were built in 1796 and situated in a hotel) the Ingram family constructed their own establishment in 1804, on the slopes of the shrubbery opposite what was the wooden pier and there the building stood for the next 75 years. That was until the council evicted them in 1879. This followed a resolution by the Southend Board of Health that stated in a letter to the Ingrams: "The occupiers of the ground near the pier , shall remove their buildings by Michaelmas next".

This order was made as the council were clearing the ground in readiness for the construction of a new brick toll-house and pier approach. For the family having occupied the site for so long having to demolish the building, must not have been taken lightly. Fortunately like Henry Absalom the Ingram's had other seaside businesses to run such as their bathing machines and their floating swimming baths. Although many associate the swimming baths attached to the pier only with the Absaloms, the fact remains that it was Thomas Ingram who first ordered the construction of "an iron floating bath" in 1869, from J.W Dudgeon of Fenchurch Street, London. At the cost £900. Later the Ingram's would sell their baths to the Absalom family.

It would be easy to conclude that the only floating baths during the late 1800s belonged to the Ingram and Absalom families, we would however be quite wrong in that assumption. There was in fact a third less well documented floating bath, that took as its name "Cleopatra". Council minutes in 1893 recommended: "That permission be given to a Mr E Ascherberg, musical publisher, of Berners Street, London to fix or moor upon the Western foreshore the Cleopatra swimming bath with means of access from the shore. For a fixed term of 3 years at the annual fee of £60 and that the corporate common seal be affixed to the necessary agreement." Quite why a musical publisher would want to own a public swimming bath, came as something of a surprise. Perhaps like the fisherman he simply wanted to supplement his income!

Marine Parade
The Golden Mile of Commerce

All along Marine Parade there are seats and shelters,
plus wash and brush up accommodation. All there are
earning a living desperate to attract the patronage of the
passing trade. They made even the most lowly of tripper
to be important, in return people would come back to
South End again and again.

Taken from a gentleman's magazine dated 1890

To understand how Henry Absalom made his fortune, we must explore the history of Marine Parade, as it turned from fishing village to a place of thriving commerce. I do not intend to quote all the relevant months or years but to give an overall impression of the changing occupations and happenings over a long period of time. I will present ordinary residents, who saw an opportunity to earn a living from the new seaside trade and some who are often mentioned in locals history books. The Vandervords being one such often quoted name. A

wealthy barge owning family with a large house on the Parade who had their own loading pier and Major General William Goodday Strutt, the area where his large house stood became know as Strutt's Parade. This gentleman is worth a mention, not only because part of the Parade was named after him, but, along

with others, he was instrumental in putting forward the ideas to the council, for the need of a wooden pier and a parish church in the heart of Southend, to serve the pastoral needs of the local population both ideas were accepted. The first wooden pier was constructed in 1829. St John's Baptist Church was completed in 1842 and still stands today serving its congregation but now dwarfed by the Palace Park Hotel and a multi storey car park near the top of Pier Hill. Buried in its graveyard, are members of the Absalom family.

Ann Absalom

To the left the Falcon Public House, on the right The Chemist on Marine Parade since 1832

Marine Parade around 1900—note the iron railings which in those days separated the carriageway from the beach

Built 1854, rebuilt in 1897 by Messrs Walker and Sons of Gravesend

The Cornucopia Public House today 2010

Although hotels like The Ship, were built in the 1700s to accommodate the visitor, pubs, cafes and coffee houses did sprung up here and there, along this strip of prime land, facing the sea. The parade did not give itself over entirely to the new excursionist. In fact it had something of an identity crisis with its large private houses and fishing cottages all standing close to one another. They shared the space running along the road, with the fruiterer, post office, hairdresser, souvenir shops and George Harrod the boot maker who later moved his business to Southchurch. Thomas Sharland the draper sold, calico, flannel petticoats,

The Falcon Pub today still in the heart of Marine Parade.
Henry Absalom was the licensed victualler in the 1870s.

The Borough Hotel—2010

dresses, corsets, hosiery and gloves from his premises near the watchmaker and jewellers shop, its owner having the grand sounding names of Fitzwilliam Sparling Dunnett. Around 1852, the first chemist shop was opened (next to where the Falcon Public House stands today). The first resident pharmacist was, Charles Montague King, born at Leigh-on-Sea, he remained there for over twenty years, before being succeeded by George Dawson, who was also a keen photographer. Many of his photographs taken around Southend during the 1900s survive today. He was one the first shops in the town to sell film for cameras.

During one period of Marine Parades history there was a large influx of Italians, who all ran businesses on the main seafront. Notably Offredi who many years later changed the family name to Offord, their bakery/restaurant, was sited at 25 Marine Parade, well into the 1970s. Pazzi Massimo and Localtella and

Marine Parade amusements 2010.

Mazzoletti were all refreshment house keepers, nearby. As was David Burles who with his wife ran the Borough Hotel (formally The Hole In The Wall) offering coffee and other beverages, the hotel is still on the promenade today. Of the many public houses along this road, two would be run by the Trigg family. Their involvement with the beer trade started with William Trigg born in Southend in 1846. After marrying, William moved to Margate, to run The Hope and Anchor but the untimely death of his wife saw him return to Southend with his young family, where he took over The Ship. Later one of his son's, went on to become the beer keeper at The Cornucopia, which still serves alcohol from its location on the corner of Hartington Road and Maine Parade today. There were other Triggs living and working along the front, during the same period but as they were all born in London, it is hard to say if they were related to the Southend branch. Peter Trigg was listed as the licensed victualler of the Forresters Arms and a "fly proprietor". I freely admit I was totally puzzled by this so called occupation, but research provided an answer, a fly was a horse drawn carriage for hire, so a fly proprietor was generally the owner of several of these carriages, employing cabbies to drive them. They would have offered the tripper a ride out to Shoeburyness and back on what was in the late 1800s/1900s a very busy single track with other cabbies plying for trade from the thousands of people thronging the area during bank holidays.

Living in Grantully House on Marine Parade in 1904, was George Myall, a Lloyds agent, whose family could trace their roots way back in the town. His son – another George - could be found at number 23, managing refreshment rooms. William Myall (born 1828) lived there in 1851 and was a mariner, he is buried in St John's churchyard. The Myalls' stayed on in the area and could still be found living and working near the seafront as boat builders and whitebait merchants in the 1930s.

I must not neglect but cannot name all the fisherman and waterman living along Marine Parade over the years, keeping alive the original purpose of the whole area.

In 1892 the council received a complaint that the Salvation Army, were congregating at the bottom of Pier Hill, the matter was referred to the Town Clerk with the authority to remove the cause for complaint! It hardly seems possible that the Salvation Army was causing a problem, that would result in their being moved on. Better news of this splendid organisation came in 1894, when they were given permission to hold services on Strutt's Green during the summer months.

In time the single track along Marine Parade was widened and the small area of grass, between the road and beach, where cricket was played and stalls were erected during the busy summer months disappeared. So did the private houses and general stores that had occupied prime sites along the road. Gradually the whole area was taken over by souvenir shops, amusement arcades, restaurants selling fish and chips, pie and mash and more and more pubs to quench the trippers thirst. The pier got longer and its trains were no longer drawn by horses. Hem lines of the ladies rose from sweeping the pavement to barely covering the thigh and in the 1950s/60s Southend was more associated with "kiss me quick hats", (which the author's parents used to manufacture), and mods and rockers invaded the town on their scooters and motor bikes.

Today (2010) Marine Parade is undergoing a major regeneration programme, as work begins on creating a huge promenade with state of the art lighting and a fountain as a centre piece (a fountain once stood on Strutt's Green). Southend-on-Sea continues to attract locals and visitors, to stroll along Marine Parade to take in its atmosphere and have fun. The major changes that have taken place in the last 300 years would make the area totally unrecognisable to the gentry who first came to take the waters in the 1700s.

Marine Parade 1963

Bathing Machines
Modesty Protectors

Bathing machines first appeared on the beaches of England in the 1700s. Small wooden boxes on wheels, or canvas stretched over a frame, they were a strange but necessary commodity, playing an integral role in the etiquette surrounding sea bathing during that period. The earliest pictorial reference to them, can be found hanging on the wall of the Scunthorpe Public Library. An engraving dated 1736, by the artist John Setterinton, it depicts a bathing machine being drawn by two horses, across a vast expanse of sand, towards the surf. Other resorts soon followed Scunthorpe's example and these new fangled changing boxes , would soon appear on beaches around the country, including South End.

The advent of bathing machines, were developed to cater for the growing

THORPE BAY.

BATHING AT THORPE BAY.

number of people , who wanted to bathe in the sea, not for fun but for purely medicinal purposes. The type of person who choose to indulge in this new fad , were royalty and the upper classes, who previously would have visited one of the many inland spars, such as the one at Leamington . They now choose to follow the dictate of a Doctor Richard Russell, a physician born in Sussex in 1687. The learned gentleman wrote and published a book in 1725 , entitled " Use of seawater in the diseases of the glands" In it he extolled the virtues of not only immersing the whole of one's body in the sea , but advocated drinking the water in large quantities . His publication was widely read and encouraged many to follow his ideals, which on paper presented no problems, but in Georgian and Regency times, both men and women swam naked.... Bathing machines solved part of the problem, in allowing the bather to undress in private, but in order to leave the box and enter the sea without being seen, required speed and agility on the part of the individual. Even though in the early days large canvas umbrellas were strategically placed as the lady entered the water, this did not always spare her blushes. Help was at hand, when in 1750 Benjamin Beale a Quaker living in Margate, provided a solution. A breeches and glove maker by profession, he designed and manufactured a huge canvas awning which could be attached to the back door . When the person inside was ready to enter the sea, the awning was pulled opened and stood like a large tent over the area in which the swimmer (usually women) would take their dip. They would return to their changing box unobserved , having enjoyed complete privacy throughout their time in the water. The inventor of this awning was himself an owner of several bathing machines that stood on the beach in his home town in Kent. And no doubt proved to be a good supplement to his income, during the summer months. The first machines that appeared on the sands at South End used Beale's simple but effective invention.

The design of Bathing machines changed little in 150 years, except that canvas sides and the awning would disappear, when swimming costumes were introduced during the Victorian age. The all wooden variety proved to be the more practical and durable. Looking more like sentry boxes, they stood 4 feet off the ground, balanced on top of their large wheels, necessitating the need for

In the background the old wooden pier

Bathing machines at Westcliff-on-Sea

a small stepladder to be able to access the inside, which measured 6 feet in both width and length. The ceiling height was a standard 8 feet, into the peaked roof , would sometimes had a small unglazed opening, to provide some light for the interior. Other machines had small windows high up in one of the wooden walls. Once inside the prospective bather would find a small bench, a flannel dress and two towels, later there would be swimming costumes that could be hired along with the bathing machine. These costumes became more and more ostentatious and covered the person from head to toe, which must have made movement in the water quite difficult. As to how the exterior of these changing facilities were decorated, was entirely down to the owners of the vans or the concessionaires. Many were painted in bright colours or covered in bold coloured wide stripes in order to attract customers. Some rather enterprising individual covered theirs in advertisements , to in bring in more revenue. Henry Absalom was quite restrained in how his machines were displayed. He simply had "ladies and children only" with his name underneath, in bold lettering on the sides of his vans.

I feel that at this point I cannot continue with the history of these machines without mention of "dippers" these ladies were much in evidence as the majority of ladies could not swim. Their task was simply to hold their customers tightly in their arms and dip them 3 times in the water and then return them safely to the steps of their changing boxes. Usually the wives of fisherman they were strong and used to the outdoor life. The most famous of these was a Mrs Glasscock, who was the first established guide or dipper, beginning her long association with the profession, in the late 1700;s. Later her advertisements would announce " that for the past 28 years she had attended families of distinction amongst which was Princess Caroline of Wales" Of course Mrs Glasscock was not alone in providing these services.

For the owners of these machines business was brisk because changing on the beach was forbidden by law, in 1898 Southend council declared in their minutes:

> Bathing is prohibited from the beach or shore between the
> Hours of six in the morning and nine at night- except from
> a Bathing machine.

In Southend-on-Sea there were many others like Ingram and Absalom, who had bathing machines at various times and different positions along the promenade,

that stretched from Westcliff to Shoeburyness.

Joseph Page
Emma Clark
George Davis
Robert Osborne
Edward Allen and the
Sparrow family.

One last name to mention, is Mark Brand, who in 1917 fell foul of the law, which governed his licence. One of the rules stated quite clearly ,that at all times a small rowboat was to be fully equipped , ready for any emergency that might occur. Brand having failed to comply with this regulation, was responsible for the death of a lady , who had rented one of his bathing machines. Having entered the water ,the poor woman got into difficulties and drowned .(we must remember that most people could not swim so the boat was an important necessity). He was fined and his licence cancelled for the rest of the season.

For all the bathing machine owners there were strict guidelines on how they operated their machines along the seafront at Southend. Most of the land and shore line had originally belonged to the Lord of The Manor, Daniel Scratton. This was sold and the busy sea front now come under the borough council . Each year all owners of bathing machines had to apply for a new licence, which came at a cost, to operate for the coming season. They were expected to keep the area around their pitch neat and tidy and the bathing machines to be cleaned on a regular basis. With a good living to be made during the summer months and in order to attract the most customers, they would no doubt have complied with these regulations to ensure good trade.

By 1910, when the rules on mixed bathing were relaxed and for the first time men and women could be seen on the same beach, the demand for bathing machines began to fall. Even though the law governing changing on the beach, was not repealed until the 1940s. Although some tried to get round this problem by wearing large Macintoshes in order to use them as their own personal mini changing booths. Councils soon

Bathing costumes 1920/30s

caught on to this habit and charged them a fee in a bid to discourage such behaviour. Bathing machines were still much in evidence however throughout the 1920's and 30's but not in the great numbers there had been before the first world war. Gradually some of the old machines were turned into beach huts with chairs and tea making facilities inside, but on Chalkwell beach in Westcliff, right up to 1950;s there were small changing boxes and tents for hire for those wishing to still observe some form of modesty when changing for a swim.

Circa 1858

Henry Absalom
1827 - 1904
A Life Of Toil And Reward
Humble Beginnings

Henry Absalom was born at the South End of Prittlewell in 1827, the son of Henry Absalom and Ruth Carvell. For reasons unexplained, Henry would use his mother's surname on two official documents, during his lifetime. First his wedding certificate and later his last will and testament. Although it was common practice in those days, for a son to take his mothers name, you would usually expect it to be shown as Henry Carvell Absalom. Quite why he chose to use Carvell on these two quite significant documents and not his father's, I cannot answer, but throughout his life Henry was known as an Absalom and this was the name recorded on his death certificate.

Cottages still standing today (2010) in a quiet mews opposite the Kursaal. Here two of Henry's uncles lived with their families in the 1800s.

Life for Henry, his sister Catherine and brother William (mentioned in Path to Prosperity) would have been hard, as in the early 1800s the area was quite poor and it would be sometime before lower South End, became a popular destination for trippers and holidaymakers. These visitors would bring much needed revenue and employment to the area and turn the once sleepy hamlet into a bustling seaside town. For both his brother and sister there would be marriage and children. Catherine married one James Edward Johnson in 1852, giving birth the following year to a son Edward. Although Catherine and James would go on to have more children, their first born was left in the care of his Absalom grandparents. In 1865 Ruth died from a disease of the brain, at the early age of just 56, leaving grandson Edward in the care of her husband who outlived her by some 24 years. Edward did not follow the family tradition of fishing nor did he become involved with the seaside trade, instead he went on to be a carpenter, living with his family in Southend for many years. For Catherine, his mother, who was widowed in 1878, through necessity she became a boarding house keeper in Scratton Road, until her death in 1904.

Henry senior, wife Ruth and their children, had a cottage, at number 2 Grovenor Place, Marine Parade (now demolished) in the 1840s, with extended members of the Absalom family living close by, including one of Henry's sisters, Charlotte married to Benjamin Johnson, the local boot maker. Living so close to the River Thames and with so few opportunities in those days, it is hardly surprising that Henry and his sons, earned a living as watermen or fishermen. In later years Henry (1827) would see that the River Thames offered more, than just a life working on the water. This foresight would be the beginning of a long road that would lead him to success as an entrepreneur.

Grovenor Place, Marine Place, note The Ship Hotel to the right.

Bailiff To Bathing Machines, Marriage and Children

Henry Absalom
1827—1904

Henry left home and took lodgings locally, by the time he was in his twenties, fishing was still his main occupation and would remain so for sometime. In 1854 he married Sarah Hawkins, who was born in North Newton in Somerset, the daughter of a farmer. According to the first census after their marriage, their first born was Mary Jane, her birth date given as 1850.

Sarah Absalom
1829—1904

It is however more likely that she was Sarah's daughter. Henry and Sarah went on to have five children of their own, three sons and two daughters. Hannah died young, but their remaining children George, Harry, Alice and Ernest reached adulthood and beyond (more of them later). With a growing family and no doubt a need for extra income it is after 1854 that Henry's path diverges. First he was employed as a bailiff for the then lord of the manor Daniel Scratton, overseeing his land in both Prittlewell and Milton parishes. By 1871 Henry is shown as the licensed victualler of the Falcon Public House on Marine Parade. Previously a private residence, it had been converted to cope with the ever growing demand for more accommodation and beer parlours for the masses, that were now converging on Southend-on-Sea during the summer months. The Falcon advertised itself as offering "ales, stouts, and good accommodation for private families"

During the Absaloms time at The Falcon they rented a three bedroom cottage close by, as there was no available living space for the family in the pub. At this point in time Henry was not the great property speculator he would soon become. Never one to stand still, around the same period that Henry was managing the public house, he was also buying into the ever increasing demand for bathing machines. Changing on the beach was against the law and with so many people wanting to take a dip in the sea, there would often be queues for these changing boxes. Henry had invested in a golden opportunity.

The Falcon, Marine Parade 1870s

1872, records show his application to Daniel Robert Scratton Esquire (who at that time also owned much of the foreshore as well as the land around lower South End) for the renewal of a licence, "One pound two shillings and sixpence to stand 9 bathing machines on the beach, between the jetty on the Esplanade, from below the centre with the shrubbery. Where they will stand out until October".

In 1877 as well as his other enterprises, Henry is again listed as working for Daniel Scratton, but this time as the foreman of his fisheries in Lower South End, by the late 1880s Henry is advertising himself as an oyster merchant. Yet another string to his bow! Oyster beds were first cultivated in Southchurch around 1700 but due to pollution they were abandoned by 1830, the only remaining oyster beds at that time in the area, were at Chalkwell Beach, about a mile along the shore out of South End. These oyster beds only lasted until 1890.

The families time as publicans, was short lived, as Henry's bathing machines and other seaside businesses began to dominate his working life and help make his fortune. Marine Parade at this time was an expanding and thriving community and he was at its very heart. Henry's life revolved completely around the golden mile that attracted thousands of visitors during the summer months.

For those who have written before about Henry Absalom there is always included with the narrative a photograph of his large floating baths moored by the pier. As I have shown earlier in this book it was not as many thought an original idea of Henry's but that of Thomas Ingram. To the reader it might seem strange that people would want to swim in these iron floating baths, which by today's standards were quite poor. Considering that it was easy enough for individuals to enter the water from the foreshore, the baths popularity, might seem strange. What these floating contraptions offered was a swim regardless of the tide. When the tide was out you would have been able to walk on the mud to the baths, when the tide was in you would have been rowed out in a small boat, having no doubt queued for sometime for your turn. Both Ingram and Absalom hired out swimming costumes to their patrons and these garments would be rinsed and hung out to dry after use, until needed again by the next customer.

Interior of Ingleside
38 Pleasant Road

At some point Henry purchased his own floating baths, which are known to have been moored off Western Esplanade, but as to their size, cost or when they were actually built is unclear. What is known however is that in 1892, Southend Council "resolved to recommend the renewal of the licence between themselves and Henry Absalom for his floating baths on the foreshore". Two years later the council increased the fee for this licence from £3 3s 0d to £5 5s 0d and also increased the cost of standing his bathing machines on the foreshore from 10/s to £1. These were peak years for visitors to Southend and no doubt the corporation could see that business was brisk and knew that increases could be met. A step to far by the local council in 1898, however resulted in a joint letter of protest from Henry and Thomas Ingram when they wrote to the council asking them to reconsider their decision to

increase their rent for their floating baths to some £200 per annum. Their protest was in vain and the decision was not overturned. What this information showed, was that there was enough business for both Absalom and Ingram to be operating their swimming baths during the same period.

As Henry's various businesses continued to thrive and provide him with a good income, he applied to the Southend Board of Health, in 1887 to build a house in Pleasant Road for himself and wife Sarah. The architect was Henry Poston of the city of London. When number 38 was completed the couple took up residence and remained there until both passed away. Today a small block of flats stands on the site of the Absalom house known as "Ingleside".

In 1897, Henry drew up his last will and testament which showed just how successful he had become. Not only with bathing machines and baths but he also owned quite a number of properties just off Marine Parade. To son Harry he bequeathed his bathing machines, winches and other appliances, connected with them, Ernest was given the floating baths with mooring chains, boats etc. To his wife Sarah, all of his real estate, but on her death numbers 43-45-47 to pass to his son George. The eight cottages in Pleasant Row plus number 39 Pleasant Road would be held by trustees for the maintenance of his daughter Alice or her children if necessary. Other properties held in Pleasant Road , numbers 23-37 to pass to his son Harry, with number 38 Pleasant Road to be given to his youngest son Ernest, as well as two properties in York Road Southend. Premises on Marine Parade had been sold prior to his will being written. With so many cottages and houses in his possession, the rent from his tenants would have provided a good income. From such humble beginnings Henry was able to lift himself from a life as a poor fisherman, because he was hard working and ready to embrace all the opportunities, that came his way at a time of great social change. For a man who could neither read nor write his success was quite remarkable.

Henry Absalom died on the 15th March 1904, at the house he had had built to his specifications, in Pleasant Road. How different from the small fisherman's cottages he lived in as a child and later a young man. Just eight days after Henry's demise his wife Sarah passed away.

Fisherman to Entrepreneur
1827—1904

Henry Absalom's journey from fisherman to seaside entrepreneur played a major part in Southend-on-Sea's history as a seaside resort. The Absalom's were a prominent family in their time. Today there is nothing to show the visitor the important role he had played during its formative years.

Family Connections
George Absalom
1856 -1907

George followed one of the family traditions by working on the Thames during most of his adult life and was registered as a boat owner up until 1890. After this date he is to be found on the foreshore with his father and brother as a bathing machine proprietor. In 1898 he married an Alice Gateson in Hendon. The bridegroom was 43 the bride just 28 years old. The couple lived first in St Leonards Road, Southend , later moving to Southchurch Avenue. George and Alice had just one child, a son, Henry Leslie born in 1900, unfortunately George did not live long enough to see his son grow into an adult as he died just seven years later, aged 51. Henry Leslie and his mother Alice remained in the town for many years with Henry marrying in 1922 to a Lily Ball. Their daughter Joan was born the following year. Alice Absalom passed away in 1930 and soon after Henry and his family moved to Hastings, in East Sussex, where the family remained. Henry died in 1976, Lily in 1979 and their daughter Joan, who never married, passed away in 1983.

Alice Amy Absalom
1858-1929

Alice, Henry and Sarah's only surviving daughter went on to marry in 1878 one George Whistler, who was a coal agent. They began married life in Daisy Villas in Wesley Road, but within a few years had moved to Southchurch. The couple went on to have five children and through their son Fritz born in 1889, there are still Whistlers living in the Southchurch area today (2010) and maybe more through their other sons, Reginald 1883—1971 and Arthur 1884—1980 who both died still living in the Southend area. For Alice and George's daughters, Doris born in 1892 married a John Henney in 1912 and her sister Margery married late in life 1935, in Chelmsford to a William Stevens. Alice Whistler claimed to be a widow on the 1901 census but in truth her husband did not die until 1909, thankfully Alice had an income through her late father's investments which sustained her until her death in 1929.

Harry Absalom
1860-1924

Harry began his working life as a plumber and painter this was during the time he was living with his parents, at number 2 Grovenor Place. The family had moved into the cottage on Marine Parade following the death of Henry senior in 1880. Harry married Josephine Elizabeth Baker a dressmaker. In 1888, born in East Ham, she had moved down to Southend with her family to live in Scratton Road. By 1891 they had three children, Beatrice, Reginald and Marjorie. Their first two children died when in their teens.

Pier Hill

In 1891, Harry had taken on the beer house at number 39 Marine Parade, later he joined his brother George, as a bathing machine proprietor, but after 1901 there were no applications for a licence to stand his machines on the beach. 1905 found Harry living with his family at 36 Pleasant Road, which he had inherited, along with other properties from his father. Just three years later he is no longer living or working in Southend, Harry has moved with his wife Josephine and their only surviving child, Marjorie, to Brentford in Middlesex. Quite why he had given up on seaside living is unknown, perhaps the loss of his two eldest children plus the income from his houses, meant he could take early retirement! In 1916 his daughter married a Henry Palmer. Harry and Josephine remained in Brentford until their deaths in 1924. Harry first followed by his wife a few months later.

Ernest Walter Absalom
1870 -1938

Property Speculator and Floating Bath Proprietor

Ernest was the last of Henry and Sarah's children and was to prove to be the most industrious and succeed in business. As early as 1893, when he was just 23 years old, he brought a property on Brewery road, known as Minerva house.

Allen family wedding
far right front row Ernest Absalom

Having also married that year to Elizabeth Amelia Allen, this was quite likely, their first home together, later they moved to Heygate Avenue. Elizabeth's father George was a builder and would work with his son in law on various building projects from 1895, when Ernest submitted plans to the council to build three shops and houses on Marine Parade and in 1896, he applied for permission to construct five houses in York Road Southend. In 1909 a letter to a solicitor, Arthur Thorne showed that maybe Ernest had overstretched his finances the letter stated: "I acknowledge to have received from you (Thorne) twelve pounds, thirteen shillings and four pence upon security of deposit of a silver coffee pot, cream jug and sugar basin and further charge my freehold properties on Marine Parade as collateral". As Ernest continued to build houses in the town, it was perhaps just a short term cash flow problem.

The baths offered the customer four to five feet of water, always available regardless of the tide. This was important to the swimmer who may have only had limited time to enjoy themselves, at the seaside and not wanting to wait for the tide to come in again some hours later. Charges were 6d per person, included in the price were the services of a rowing boat (like the one in the picture below), to take the swimmers from the shore and back when the tide was in.

The interior of Ernest Absalom's bath were quite poor when comparing them with today's standards, although they did at least offer the swimmer changing rooms to slip into their costumes, of which most would have been hired from Ernest himself. The baths did a roaring trade until their closure in 1914.

Standing to the left of the pool in a small group of people is Ernest Walter Absalom, wearing a white jacket.

No. 14164

Port of London Authority.

Certificate of Registration of River Craft.

Name of Craft _Ernest_

Description _Partly Decked Barge_

Owner's name _Ernest Walter Absolom_

Owner's address _Ingleside, Pleasant Road, Southend-on-Sea, Essex_

Owner's number _1059_

Craft number _14164_

Tonnage by measurement _143½_ tons.

Weight-carrying capacity or burden tonnage _239¼_ tons.

These are to Certify that (on payment of the sum of £ _3-11-9_) the Port of London Authority have this day registered the above-named craft as above, pursuant to the provisions of the Thames Watermen's and Lightermen's Act, 1893, as amended by the Port of London Act, 1908.

This Certificate will remain in force until the _14th_ day of _December_ 19_11_ only, unless renewed from time to time.

Dated this _14th_ day of _December_ 1910.

R. Philipson

General Manager and Secretary.

34

Ernest's life was not taken up entirely as a developer, although with the number of shops and properties he owned, organising his property empire would still have demanded a certain amount of his time to keep abreast of his many investments. Just some of the properties he owned, included five shops and dwelling houses on Marine Parade and on his father's death he inherited cottages in Pleasant Row. Later he would build houses with his father-in-law, who was a builder at numbers 13 and 14 York Road. Ernest was always looking to invest in the town with a keen interest in continuing to provide amenities for trippers and the locals looking to enjoy the delights of the seaside. The town was still a very popular destination and with improvement in travel times, thanks to the LTS Railway, many Londoner's would continue to visit Southend-on-Sea in their thousands, up until the 1960s.

In 1903 Ernest purchased the Ingram's floating baths that were moored at the most prestigious spot on the seafront, right next to the famous pier. Thomas Ingram the founder had now died and his family, for whatever reason, decided to sell their assets including the floating baths. A letter from the Ingram's stated "this day we have received from Ernest Walter Absalom the sum of £600 pounds the agreed price for the swimming baths, gear, boats and effects, plus the goodwill of the business forming part of the estate of the late Thomas Ingram". The family had originally paid £900 pounds to have the baths constructed, which were sold at a loss of some £300 pounds which of course was to Ernest's advantage. Once all legal matters were finalised, this well known Southend landmark would have "Absalom's Floating Baths" in large bold letters across the side which would have made it easy to read from the shore. The following year 1904 on the death of Henry Absalom, Ernest inherited his smaller floating baths, giving him the monopoly on the Thames at Southend.

Absalom's baths remained by the pier up to the outbreak of the First World War when due to the hostilities the council issued a notice that they must be towed away to new moorings. The pier had not only become part of the town's defences, but taking the place of where once there were floating baths would be three converted Cunard Liners to serve as prison ships, for the German prisoners who began arriving in the town during the first year of the war

The baths were due to be towed away but early in 1914 a letter was submitted to the council with regard to the baths. The following is their reply:

Western Esplanade with the new corporation open air swimming pool.

"The bathing sub committee have carefully considered letters, received from the Rev F. Dormer Pierce and Mr E. W Whitton president and Hon. Secretary respectively of St. Johns swimming club, with regard to their application for swimming facilities for their members. You asked that Mr E W Absalom might be allowed to place his baths on the foreshore west of the pier for the coming season for this purpose. In view of the improbability of the new swimming pool being constructed on Western Esplanade being open for public bathing, until late in the coming season, it is desirable that sea bathing facilities should be provided for this club representing 270 members and a large number of junior members".

The committee having agreed to the request, then laid down their conditions that the baths should remain for only one season and must be removed in the October of 1914 and that Ernest Absalom be charged a nominal rent of 10/s 6d. The baths were towed from their moorings by the pier, to the western end of Chalkwell Beach opposite the railway bridge, where they remained in situ until that autumn. This was effectively the end of the floating baths, for come the end of the war when Ernest applied for a licence, to moor the baths once more by the pier, he was refused because the new swimming pool on Western Esplanade was now completed and opened to the public. The baths were towed to a ship breaking yard at Leigh-on-Sea where they were demolished.

Pier Hill 1900s

The Pier Master and Swimming Costumes

One quite strange note in the council minuets with regard to the new swimming pool, was that the acting pier master had submitted samples of bathing costumes, which had been made by pier staff! The pier master was directed to have some of these samples washed in seawater and if the garments proved satisfactory then the council would purchase same and hire them out at the new pool. Quite whether they did prove to be of sufficient quality I cannot say.

Interior of the Corporation's new swimming baths on Western Esplanade 1920s. Construction had started on these baths in 1911, they opened in 1915.

Ernest Absalom
Husband And Father

Ernest and Elizabeth were married for 23 years before in 1916 they parted, according to the deed of separation the reason cited was "unhappy differences have arisen" This ending of their marriage was quite out of keeping with the era , as separation and divorce were most frowned upon and could make you a social outcast. Elizabeth was well provided for and was given her own home where she lived with the children of this marriage. Although separated I doubt the couple actual divorced, each lived out their lives in their respective homes. In 1938 Ernest died, his wife Elizabeth outlived him by some 12 years,

Elizabeth Absalom nee Allen

The Children

Ernest and Elizabeth had three children, Ernest Henry 1897-1911, Jack Allen 1903—1959 and Ronald George 1905—1983. Having three sons should have been a sure way to see the future of the Absalom name continued at Sounthend-on-Sea. However their eldest child Ernest died aged just 14 and middle son Jack, who remained in the town all this life, living as an adult in Boscombe Road, never married. It was left to Ronald their youngest to continue the family line and connection with the town.

Jack Allen 1903—1959, baby
Ronald George 1905—1983
Standing is Ernest Henry 1897—1911

When the time came for Ronald to earn his living it was one far removed from bathing machines and floating baths. In 1924 a letter dated the 13th March read "enclosed is the apprenticeship indenture of your son Ronald P Absalom to P Morgan Ltd Motor Engineers". Ten years later Ronald married Ethel Sawkins, the couple's first home was in Eastern Avenue, later they would move to Henley Crescent in Westcliff, where they remained until Ronald's death in 1983. The couple had a daughter Moria in 1935 and a son, Terence in 1942. He went on to be a teacher at one of the local schools, Cecil Jones and later qualified as a pilot at Southend Airport.

Due to Ronald Absalom donating photographs of his family to Southend Museum I was able to include in this book, not only pictures of the Absalom children when young, but of Henry Absalom himself, one of our seaside entrepreneurs.

From Beginning To End

Henry Absalom's journey from fishermen to seaside entrepreneur played a major role in Southend's development as a seaside resort. From offering the masses bathing machines, swimming baths, food, accommodation and public houses to drink the beverages of the day they contributed to the success of the town The Absalom's were a prominent family in Southend covering the period from the 1860s through to the 1920s. Apart from the income earned from the trippers they also acquired an impressive property portfolio Today there is nothing to show the visitor that they had once been an integral part of Southend-on-Sea's development as a holiday destination

The Kursaal in its early days

The Jaquests

Marylebone — Southend-on-Sea

1854 — Present Day

Surname Jaquest

As the name would suggest, its origin is French. Taken from the old French personal name of "Jaques". There are also two Latin forms of "Jacobus" and "Jacomous". In England or Scotland the more familiar use of the name is "Jack" where it is used as a Christian or first name rather than a surname.

When the first poll tax was introduced in England, surnames became necessary as the government of the day introduced personal taxation. It is thought that the name Jacques was introduced into England as early as 1275 and since that time has continued to change and develop with modern variations such as Jacquet – Jaquiss and Jaquest.

Researching the surname in England for this book, the earliest references offered were two Jaquest marriages, in Bedfordshire. First was a William in 1640, then in 1668 the wedding of an Alice Jaquest. The next reference showed another marriage this time taking place in Northamptonshire in 1756. By the 1800s records showed only a small number of people living in the London area, with the surname Jaquest, the majority were still to be found in the Bedford area with increasing numbers shown in Northampton. Famous for its shoemaking since the middle ages, I considered that perhaps the Jaquests and their extended families had moved to the area as it seemed to offer a good source of employment. This was found not to be the case as the 1841 census showed only one Jaquest giving his occupation as shoemaker. In keeping with the times the rest worked on the land or in factories, there were only two exceptions. One

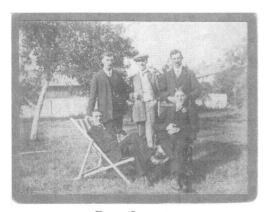

Essex Jaquests

was listed as a butcher, the other a poulterer. By the 1900s there would be more Jaquests living in the London area than anywhere else.

Today the surname can still be found in London and other parts of the country, but not Essex. Although John Jaquest had three sons only one had children and they being four daughters the surname disappeared with their marriages.

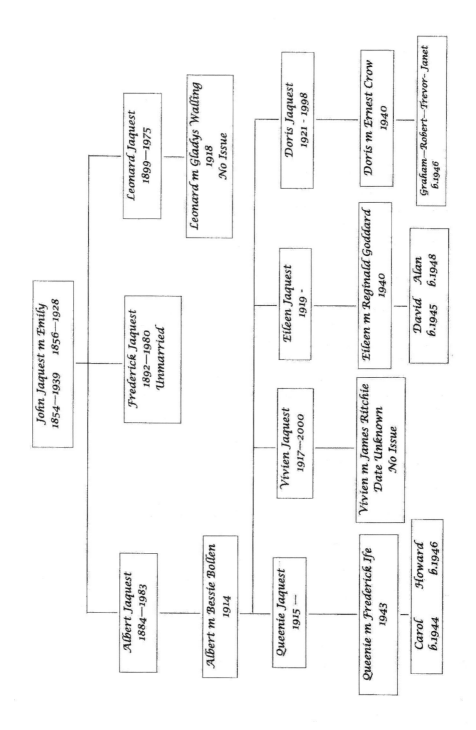

John Jaquest m Emily
1854—1939   1856—1928

Albert Jaquest
1884—1983

Frederick Jaquest
1892—1980
Unmarried

Leonard Jaquest
1899—1975

Albert m Bessie Bollen
1914

Leonard m Gladys Walling
1918
No Issue

Queenie Jaquest
1915 —

Vivien Jaquest
1917—2000

Eileen Jaquest
1919 -

Doris Jaquest
1921 - 1998

Queenie m Frederick Ife
1943

Vivien m James Ritchie
Date Unknown
No Issue

Eileen m Reginald Goddard
1940

Doris m Ernest Crow
1940

Carol
b.1944

Howard
b.1946

David
b.1945

Alan
b.1948

Graham—Robert—Trevor-Janet
b.1946

John Jaquest
1854—1939

William Jaquest
|
John Jaquest & Emily

John Jaquest

John Jaquest began his working life as a bricklayer, born in Marylebone in London in 1854, the family had been in the area since 1813, when his grandfather (another John) was born in Paddington and gave his occupation as plasterer. At that time Paddington and Marylebone were separate metropolitan boroughs, with quite different identities. Marylebone owed its character to Georgian buildings, which were constructed around 1720, whilst Paddington did not fully develop for another century. But both areas have a number of well known landmarks, such as the Grand Union Canal, Regent's Park and home to London's first underground railway. John (1854) had two brothers who, like himself, worked in the building industry. Their father William, like his father before him, was a plasterer, a skill which he passed on to his son Benoni (who died young, aged 33 in 1895). A third son, another William was a stonemason. In 1891 John and his wife were living at 39 Capland Street, Marylebone, being without work during this period, it was left to his wife Emily, whose occupation was given as "general shopkeeper" to provide the family with an income. A family that would increase in the next few years to three sons, Leonard, Frederick and Albert and three daughters Lily Alice and Daisy.

The Jaquest family moved to Southend in 1901, the reason for this move might have been due to

Emily Jaquest

45

John Jaquest centre

the amount of building work going on in the Borough during this period. With new housing estates being built in various parts of the town or it may simply have been the desire to move to a cleaner and safer environment as some parts of Marylebone were crowded and noisy. At first John Jaquest continued earning his living as a builder, records show that he was instrumental in building a bungalow for a Mr Willis in Branksome Road, Southchurch but at some point in 1908 he made the decision to take over a fish shop previously run by a William Foster. The shops address was given as 12 Kursaal Pavement and this would suggest that his premises were very near the newly opened building with its famous silver dome. The Kursaal offered an arcade with amusements, a billiard room, dance hall and a circus! The fish shop/restaurant was in an ideal position to serve the locals living on housing estates nearby and visitors with fresh fish to take away or to enjoy a meal inside. By 1913 the shop was still open but by now its address was given as 3 Victoria Place, East Parade, although it was not the shop that had moved, but because the area was being developed and new buildings were going up all along the seafront hence a new postal address. At number 2 East Parade was a lady called Mary Bollen, a widow from Rotherhithe who was running her premises as a dining room. Later John's son Albert, would marry Bessie Bollen, daughter of Mary. Within a few years the address became one we are more familiar with today (2009), Eastern Esplanade.

The business continued to trade through the First World War, during which time John's sons served Queen and country. Remarkably all survived. In 1920 John Jaquest was to be found at number 17 Eastern Esplanade where he had opened a restaurant called The Beehive, having given up the fish shop at number 3. By

Envelope, date stamped 1908

1925 John and his wife Emily had retired and were living at 15 Stanley Road, Southend. For Emily retirement was to be short lived as she died at the beginning of 1928. Her husband remarried later that year to a Mary Will. John Jaquest passed away in 1939 just before the outbreak of the Second World War.

Albert John Jaquest
1884—1983

Albert & Bessie Jaquest
|
Queenie—Vivien—Eileen—Doris

Frederick Jaquest in background with two of Albert's daughters.

Albert Jaquest was to spend his middle years living and working on the seafront at 23 Eastern Esplanade, Southend-on-Sea. First as a greengrocer, before changing his premises into a restaurant called The Sunflower, then working as a caterer from his seafront address. These occupations were in sharp contrast to his early working life and family roots in London.

Born in Middlesex in 1884, Albert moved with his parents John and Emily and his siblings, to live in Marylebone, London in 1890 where he attended Lisson Grove school until he was 12, when he left to begin work as a boot boy in the Edgware Road. He would move on to become a shop assistant, although he spent the majority of his time making the tea and cleaning up. For this he was paid the princely sum of half a crown a week. To supplement his earnings he cleaned the family home before leaving for work and added an extra penny to his pocket. But not content with his lot he decided to change course and follow his father and brothers

Albert Jaquest greengrocer's shop

47

into the building trade which, as Marylebone was expanding at the time, provided him with plenty of work for his new found skill of bricklaying. One of his first jobs was converting houses into flats at Westbourne Terrace in London. These large houses had been built in the 1840s, but with a growing population in the area more accommodation was needed and these large blocks of terraced houses were perfect for conversion. When work was completed on this project he moved on to The University College Hospital in Gower Street. Originally opened in 1828 as a small dispensary, it had continued to grow and expand for years, adding new buildings and wards to cope with the ever increasing demand on its services.

In 1900 there came a change in Albert's working life as he found employment on the railway as an improver. Trains in those days were of course steam driven. Working a 60 hour week he was paid 8s 4d. One of his memories during this period was following the death of Queen Victoria, one of England's longest reigning monarchs, he stood and watched her funeral train go past on its way to Windsor. Another major event he witnessed was the first car to be seen driving on the streets of London.

For Albert, life in London with his family had its routines, they would all attend church on a Sunday at 6am. And every day with his sister Daisy he would walk to the bakers in the Edgware Road to buy stale bread for 3d and on a Friday he would he would queue at the local poultry shop to buy giblets for the family's dinner.

In 1901 the whole family moved to Southend-on-Sea, searching for a better life and the cleaner air offered by the Thames. With his brother Fred, Albert found a job as a butcher's boy for Baileys in the Southchurch Road. They would make their rounds in a horse and cart and were each paid 5s 6d per week. The role of delivery boy didn't last long, as Albert moved on to manual work for Southend Corporation laying concrete slabs along

John Jaquest and his son Albert in uniform

the seawall. This was part of the general development of the area at that time, to improve facilities provided for the growing number of visitors who still came to the resort for holidays and days out.

The family had resided at various addresses when they first started living in Southend, it was not until 1908 when John Jaquest (Albert's father) brought his first property on the seafront, that the Jacquet's laid down more permanent roots. This was the beginning of Albert's long association with Eastern Esplanade, but it would still be a few more years before he opened his shop.

Next door to the Jaquest shop was a dining room whose proprietor was a Mary Bollen. Like the Jaquests, Mary had lived in London where she was a shopkeeper, but on the death of her husband had moved down to Southend with her family, which included daughter Bessie, who would later meet and marry Albert Jaquest. Working for R. A. Jones the Jewellers in Southend High Street, Bessie later took lodgings in Lancaster Gardens with another female employee of the well known jewellers.

By the time Albert and Bessie were getting married in 1914, Mary Bollen had left her dining room on Eastern Esplanade to run the Rose and Crown Public House in Chelmsford which was regarded as one of the few public houses in the area as a decent place for respectable working class people to enjoy a drink. The wedding took place in Chelmsford Cathedral and the day was shared with

Albert and Bessie's wedding day
(couple to the right)

Bessie's sister Nellie who married an Alfred Wakeling. Their joint reception was of course held in the Rose and Crown.

Following the wedding Albert and Bessie moved to Sutton Road, Southend, next to All Saints Church. Later they would live in Cromwell Road before finally settling in 1916 at 1 Wellington Place, where they opened a fruiterers, which Bessie was left to run as these changes to their lives came during the First World War.

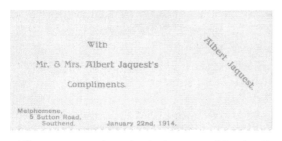

With

Mr. & Mrs. Albert Jaquest's

Compliments.

Melphomene,
5 Sutton Road,
Southend.   January 22nd, 1914.

Albert Jaquest enlisted in the army, as did many others during this period, he was first in the East Kent Regiment, but was then transferred to the Essex Regiment Royal Irish Rifles in which he served until the end of the war. During the Great War Albert managed to obtain leave and in the first of his four daughters were born. Queenie Bessie 1915 – Vivien Myrtle 1917. Two more daughters were to follow later Eileen Nellie 1919 and Doris Muriel 1921. For Albert and Bessie their family was now complete.

By 1920 the Jaquest's address had become 22 Eastern Esplanade where they continued selling their fruit and vegetables until 1934, but they lived next door at number 23. In 1927 Albert applied for permission to build accommodation above the shop making the two

The greengrocers property to the left, in 1927 building work on accommodation above the shop having just begun.

The Sunflower

properties into one large living space. In 1934 the shop was converted into a restaurant which he called The Sunflower. The name was taken from an earlier tea rooms that had stood on the beach side of Eastern Esplanade – previously Southchurch Beach Road. The tea rooms had stood adjacent to The Methodist Chapel and near The Castle Hotel. All three buildings would eventually be demolished, the original

Albert and Bessie at
3 Chester Avenue, Southend
1950s

Sunflower was first in the early 1900s to make way for road widening. Next came The Castle, but having been taken down it was to be re-built further along the Esplanade where it still stands today, serving drinks and offering accommodation to visitors. The chapel survived well into the 1920s, by which time it was no longer a place of worship, but used as storage space.

Albert was to manage his Sunflower restaurant for just five years, like his brother Leonard, he catered mainly for the town's visitors with traditional English fare although he also served those working locally, in offices or shops. After the Second World War was declared it soon became obvious that keeping his premises open was going to prove impossible. With permits needed to enter the town, as the area was considered a high security risk because of its close proximity to the River Thames, visitors were few and far between. And with many of the locals already having been evacuated to other parts of the country, Albert and Bessie were forced to close their restaurant and with their now grown up daughters moved to North Finchley. Unfortunately this proved to be out of the frying pan and into the fire as the bombing in London and surrounding areas grew worse as the war continued.

After two years away the Jaquest's returned home and Albert embarked on a new career as a caterer, offering to organise birthday parties, wedding receptions and anniversary celebrations for the locals. Using the site of the old restaurant and when demand was high, the family's large living room upstairs. Albert continued in this new role for the next four years.

In 1946 number 23 Eastern Esplanade was put up for sale, but it was to stand empty for the next twelve months before being sold. The sale brought to an end

Albert and Bessie

nearly forty years association with Eastern Esplanade, which began with his father's fish shop. Albert and Bessie were by now in their fifties could afford to retire and spend more time with their family and growing number of grandchildren, who would fill their house number 3 Chester Avenue, in the summer months, because it was so near the beach. Albert was a Freemason like his brother Leonard and his retirement gave him more time to devote to the lodge and to look after their property investments.

For Bessie Jaquest there was to be only eight years of retirement as she died in 1954. Albert lived on alone in their house until the 1960s when his daughter Myrtle, now a widow, returned home from America. Moving in with her father she remained there until his death in 1983. Albert John Jaquest was just two months and ten days away from his one hundredth birthday.

Albert with his four daughters 1954

Frederick Jaquest
1892 -1980

John & Emily Jaquest
|
Frederick Jaquest (unmarried)

Frederick as a young man

Frederick like his brothers and sisters, was born in London, coming to Southend-on-Sea when he was around nine years old. As a young man he took various jobs to earn money, including time at his brother Albert's greengrocers working as a shop assistant, but Frederick unlike his brothers did not embark on a life as a shopkeeper or become a proprietor of a café/restaurant. Instead his chosen career stayed loyal to a long held Jaquest family tradition of working in the building trade, where the male members of the line had been plasterers, stonemasons and bricklayers. Frederick became a carpenter and when called up during the First World War his occupation was listed as carpenter improver and his address was given as 20 Eastern Esplanade, where the family had their various businesses. Leonard joined the Queen's Royal West Surrey Regiment transferring later to the labour corps where he was part of a squad of men, who were called upon to fill in craters on the roads damaged by enemy bombing.

Their picks and shovels were also used to dig tunnels as and when required. Far from being a safe option they were often near the front line and in as much danger as those in the trenches. Remarkably like Leonard and Albert, Frederick survived the Great War.

When the war ended in 1918 he was discharged and he came home to resume his life and return to his peacetime occupation of carpentry. Unlike his siblings, Frederick was the only one who never married. He died in 1980 aged 88 still a resident of Southend-on-Sea.

Frederick on the left, Albert in the middle and Leonard on the right at a family gathering

Leonard William Jaquest
1899—1975

John & Emily Jaquest
|
Leonard Jaquest m Gladys Walling
No Issue

Leonard Jaquest and his wife Gladys Walling

Leonard William Jaquest was the middle son of Emily and John Jaquest, like his siblings (including three sisters) he was born in London in 1889, where he lived for the first twelve years of his life. When the family moved to Southend in 1901 he took a variety of jobs, but it was to be following the First World War that Leonard worked for his brother, who had a greengrocers and his father John (previously a builder) who had a fish shop on what had become known as Eastern Esplanade (previously East Parade).

When first called up in 1914, Leonard was living at number 6 Marine Parade, which was as it is today in the heart of what was called Lower Southend. But later his service records showed that he gave his address as number 20 Eastern Esplanade.

During the First World War, Leonard served at Passchendaele where there were over 310,000 casualties, who had fought for months in the most dreadful conditions. He would later tell his nephew Patrick Hendry that the dreadful memories of that time, never left him. As a member of the Army Service Corps whose responsibilities lay in supplying the troops with food, water, clothing and fuel, Leonard's role of a driver was to ensure that these essential items reached the troops.

When the war ended in 1918 he married Gladys Irene Walling. Born in 1895 in Camberwell, her parents were Ebenezer Carolous and Sarah Walling both of whom were born in Devon. Their occupations were lodging house keeper, it

*The Star Café number
3 Eastern Esplanade*

was perhaps here that their daughter learned some of the skills that would be needed to run the restaurants with her husband. Although her sisters helped with their parents lodging house, Gladys was a dressmaker's assistant prior to her marriage.

Leonard joined his father at number 17 Eastern Esplanade, where they worked together running The Beehive. The restaurant offered traditional English fare, soup, roast dinners, steamed puddings, cheese and biscuits all at a reasonable price. As well as lunches, afternoon teas were also available. On offer were bread and butter, jam, shrimps, cakes and buns and cups of tea, served at the table from teapots, never from urns! In 1925 John Jaquest retired and in that same year number 3 Eastern Esplanade became vacant. Leonard took over the establishment which had previously been where his father had run his fish business. These small premises were turned into the Star Dining Rooms. The name was taken from The Star Restaurant and Coffee house which had occupied the site in 1901 when its

Leonard behind the counter

proprietor had been one Herbert Sawkins. The coffee house only traded for two years before new owners and a change of use came into effect.

The third and final business was taken on in 1935, sharing its name with the restaurant at number 17, but number 24 Eastern Esplanade was a much bigger site offering accommodation for up to 400 people. It was ideal for coach parties visiting the town, offering a large assembling ground opposite the restaurant where the customers could rejoin their coach having enjoyed their meal at The Beehive.

The period between the two wars was an extremely busy time for Leonard and Gladys. The town was full during the summer months with holidaymakers and

The blackboard to the left announces that two hundred children are having dinner and tea here today, supplied by the Hackney Joinery Men.

INTERIOR OF THE BEEHIVE RESTAURANT, EASTERN ESPLANADE, SOUTHEND-ON-SEA.

Leonard and Gladys enjoying a social evening at his Lodge

day trippers who took advantage of the regular steam train service and cheap fares. For the majority who came to Southend at the time, visiting the Kursaal was a must. With side shows offering diverse entertainment which included a snake charmer, the giant water ride and many other attractions, it was the place to be. With the Jaquests restaurants just around the corner from the Kursaal, they were well placed to attract customers and this they did in there hundreds. As well as catering for the visitor and large coach parties, the Beehive also offered the locals somewhere to celebrate those special occasions, such as birthdays or wedding anniversaries, either in the restaurant itself or one of the private rooms available for hire.

Leonard and Gladys, not having had children, devoted their life to building up their various business interests which included property investments. They purchased several houses around Warrior Square which they rented out. Life was not all work as Leonard was a Freemason, his lodge used to stand in Woodgrange Drive, Southend, (now a block of flats) from this there would have been meetings and social events. They also enjoyed holidays with their

good friends the Clarkes who ran the fish and chip shop not far from them on Eastern Esplanade.

When the war broke out in 1939 trading was made difficult and in time with rationing and the area being bombed many locals were evacuated to other parts of the country and it became impossible to keep The Star and Beehive restaurants open. Leaving for Derbyshire, rather than be idle while away from home they opened what was called a "peoples kitchen". These kitchens served

Leonard Jaquest sitting to the right of the stage behind him Stanley Strutt and his Orchestra

the local populace who might have been bombed out of their homes and were living in church halls until such times new accommodation could be found for them. With no cooking facilities the type of kitchens run by the Jaquests were much needed. Returning to Southend at the end of the war the couple called time on their working life on the seafront and by the late 1940s their businesses were sold. Retirement beckoned.

With more time to relax the couple joined The Southend Bowling Club which was in Victoria Avenue, where it still stands today (2010). When the club had their annual dinner dance in 1951, the Stanley Strutt Orchestra was hired for the special event and Leonard acted as MC for the evening.

When first retired Mr and Mrs Jaquest lived in Dowset Avenue. Having removed the stain glass window from above the door of The Beehive they installed it in their new home. The couple lived there until 1957 when they sold the property to the Harvey family who remained in the house until it was demolished to make way for the new duel

Telephone: 45027

Leonard W. Jaquest

36, Dowsett Avenue,
Southend-on-Sea.

carriageway in Southend. Leonard and Gladys moved to 29 St James Avenue, Thorpe Bay where they lived for the next seventeen years. Gladys died in 1974, Leonard outlived her by only a year dying in 1975 at the age of 86.

Queenie Jaquest
1915—

Albert & Bessie Jaquest
|
Queenie m Frederick Ife
|
Carol — Howard

Queenie 1st row third from left

I was introduced to Queenie Jaquest by her granddaughter Wendy Clark. We all sat in the comfortable surroundings of her retirement home so that I might gain an insight into one of the many families who had played their part in the history and development of Southend-on-Sea as a seaside resort. Her memories and the photographs she has so kindly lent me for this book, will bring alive a bygone era. —CE

Born in 1915, at Southend-on-Sea, Queenie Jaquest has witnessed great changes to the area, growing up with her siblings Vivien (1917) Eileen (1919) and Doris (1921) on the seafront, where they lived above their parents various businesses. It was during the years holiday makers and day trippers filled the town, between the two wars.

Her parents, Albert and Bessie ran their fruiterers and later The Sunflower restaurant close to where her grandfather John and uncle Leonard ran their shop and restaurants, on Eastern Esplanade (opposite to where the Sealife Centre stands today 2009). Now 95 years old Queenie's memories included her time at Brewery Road School (now Porters Grange - Lancaster Gardens). Opened in 1892 to serve the growing population to the east of the town, school hours were much like they are today. Every morning the pupils attended a "gathering" (assembly) this would be followed by the first lesson of sums, then composition, with the third lesson being geography and history. The boys and girls attending the school would go into separate classes for some of their education. Sewing and cooking were strictly for the girls whilst the boys learned how to garden. During playtime and at lunchtime the children were not allowed to mix. Girls played in one part of the playground the boys another. "Every year the school held a pound day" Queenie recalled "when we were expected to bring to school a pound of something, either sugar, fruit, flour, cheese or bread". These gifts were then given to the local church for them to distribute among the poor. This tradition continues today in many schools and is generally organised in the autumn and called Harvest Festival.

Children's Playground Eastern Esplanade 1920s

"During the summer season" Queenie told me " the trippers came to the town in their thousands" adding that if I had been there and looked towards Pier Hill all I would have seen was a mass of people heading towards the front all intent on having a good time. Which of course included food and many of them found their way to her grandfather and uncle's restaurants and later her own father's eatery The Sunflower. With their parents working long hours, their aunt Nellie (their mother's sister) was hired as housekeeper, taking charge of the general running of 23 Eastern Esplanade and looking after the four Jaquest children. Not having much of a back garden the girls spent a lot of the time on the beach opposite, where their aunt Nellie often brought them their lunch. Because of lack of space which would be enlarged in 1927 when extra rooms were added above the family shop, their aunt and her brother lived in two sheds at the back of the property "during the building work my sister Eileen and I had to walk across beams to reach our bedroom, we were petrified".

As well as the beach opposite their home, there used to be a large children's playground, full of swings, roundabouts and climbing frames. Further along was the Free Methodist Church and a few houses as well as the Castle Hotel. The church and houses disappeared many years ago but the Castle Hotel was moved further along the Esplanade where it still stands today, serving food and drink to the locals and visitors.

Bessie and two of her daughter's Queenie and Eileen

Moving onto the time when her parents were running The Sunflower and the Second World War was just around the corner Queenie told of her sister Eileen's birthday, "it was the 3rd of September 1939 and my sister had chosen that day to announce her engagement to Reginald Goddard". Far from celebrating the family found themselves huddled round the radio waiting for important news that would follow the sound of Big Ben. "The news of course" she said "was Neville Chamberlain announcing that England was at War with Germany". People on holiday simply packed up and went home, everything began to change quite quickly. The area was subject to the sound of the first air raid sirens, huge concrete blocks were built along the promenade and gas masks and identity cards were issued. Out at sea could be seen large barrage balloons, she said, "When the evacuation came from Dunkirk, the large garage to the back of our property, was used to house many of the wounded soldiers, who came back on the small fishing boats of Old Leigh leaving much needed space in the local hospital for the more seriously wounded". Eventually the Jaquest family were all evacuated to North Finchley in London, not perhaps in

Queenie and Frederick's wedding 1943

Queenie's own words the best of moves, as London was being bombed heavily every night. So the family returned home within two years. Two of Queenie's sisters had married during their time away. In 1943 Queenie married Frederick Ife at a church in Southend.

The couple went on to have two children, Howard and Carol. Howard would later go on to own The Chalkwell and Arlington function suites in Westcliff.

Carol and Howard

Queenie and Frederick, opened a café called the "Bon-eta" in the London Road, just a five minute walk from the main High Street. As well as serving hot lunches between noon and 3pm each day, they had also offered their customers breakfast and at other times, tea, sandwiches and cakes were available.

BON-ETA CAFE

130 LONDON ROAD

SOUTHEND ON SEA

PHONE 426681 PROPRIETOR MR IFE

Queenie outside the café

Today Queenie lives close to were her café stood all those years ago. Now 94 years old, she lives in comfortable surroundings, her walls covered with family photographs and time to remember a different way of life.

Queenie today 2010

Vivien Myrtle Jaquest
1917 - 2000

Albert & Bessie Jaquest
|
Vivien m James Ritchie
No Issue

*Myrtle and husband
James Ritchie*

Unfortunately I was never to meet Vivien Myrtle Jaquest but was to learn of her early years, marriage and life abroad from her sister Queenie and her great niece Wendy Clark both of whom provided me with memories and family photographs. - CE

Always known as Myrtle by the family, she grew up on the seafront with her three sisters attending the same school, Brewery Road. When the family returned to Southend during the Second World War, Myrtle worked in The Sunflower. Here she met her future husband James Abernethy Ritchie, who came into the restaurant for a meal. From Cains in Scotland, he worked for a giant timber company and when the war ended was sent to Canada to work for the company. Following him out there sometime later, Myrtle and James were to be married in Canada.

Myrtle

When her husband's job ended, they moved out to California and although a long way from home, Myrtle followed in the families footsteps and opened a modern restaurant which served fast food. Their business was called "Chicken Express".

64

Queenie and Myrtle on Southend Pier

In 1964, James Ritchie died at the relatively young age of just 43. Myrtle stayed on in America for a year or two running the Chicken Express alone, but finally around 1966 she decided to return home to England. Going to live with her father, at the house in Chester Avenue as her father Albert, was now a widower, she was to stay with him until his death a few years later.

Far from just running her father's home, Myrtle went into partnership with her sister Eileen and together they took on the running of the café in Priory Park. Throughout the 1970s they were to be found serving food, drink and ice creams during the long summer months to the many families who came to relax in one of Southend's oldest parks. The café still stands today serving the next generation of visitors where once there were Jaquests at the helm other hands now offer up refreshments to the customers.

A postcard to Myrtle on the occasion of her birthday in 1928

Having followed her family into the retail trade with the fast food restaurant in America and the café in Priory Park, Myrtle stayed close to her sisters and their families until her death in 2000.

Myrtle and Eileen Christmas 1998

Eileen Nellie Jaquest
1919—2010

Albert & Bessie Jaquest
|
Eileen Jaquest m Reginald Goddard
|
David —Alan

Albert and Bessie enjoying a walk with their daughters

I was unable to meet with Eileen (Jaquest) and Reginald Goddard, as both are now quite elderly. Still living near Southend-on-Sea, because of their advancing years, the couple now live quietly, which is in sharp contrast to their busy lives throughout their marriage, when they ran businesses together or separately.—CE

Eileen Nellie Jaquest was born just after the end of the First World War and grew up with her family above the family's shop on Eastern Esplanade. The seafront was her playground and Brewery Road School was where she gained an education.

She met her future husband in the late 1930s they announced their engagement on her birthday. It was also the day Britain declared war on Germany. Soon after the family were evacuated to London. The family stayed in London for just two years, before deciding to return to their home in Essex but during this period Eileen and Reginald took the decision to get married in Hendon in 1940. Like many couples they were separated by the war and they did not have their sons David and Alan until 1945 and 1948.

With hostilities over the couple settled down to married life in Southend and opened their first business which was a DIY shop in the London Road. The shop was just round the corner from her sister Queenie's café in Park Street and

Eileen and Queenie ready for school

near her other sister Doris' ironmongers in the London Road.

During the fifties and sixties when rock and roll began to sweep across the country, coffee bars were the place for the majority of teenagers to hang out. With their fancy coffee machines and if you were lucky, juke boxes to blare out the last Cliff Richard or Elvis Presley recordings, they were the place to be seen. Southend-on-Sea was not immune to this latest craze with the Sorrento Coffee Lounge that was opened in the High Street being the first to have that all important juke box. Others followed including Denny Knott who opened the Capri Coffee Bar in Weston Road just off the main shopping area. On the corner of Lambert and Prittlewell Street (near Victoria Station). Eileen and Reginald embraced this new fad and opened the Zanzibar Coffee bar. It had two rooms with a miniature bowling alley in the backroom. I have been unable to find out if it also had a juke box. By the 1970s Eileen was running the café in Priory Park with her sister Myrtle who had returned from America. The café sold ice creams, sandwiches, drinks and sweets much like it does today (2010).

While Eileen worked with her sister, Reginald was still running the DIY shop and for a time shared half of the floor space with his son Richard who used the area to sell confectionary.

Eileen and Reginald 2010

Eventually the couple gave up all their various businesses and decided to take life a little easier and retire. Eileen and Reginald having lived a busy working life as well as raising a family moved to Wakering to enjoy their retirement. Eileen passed April 2010.

Doris Muriel Jaquest
1921- 1998

Albert & Bessie Jaquest
|
Doris Jaquest m Ernest Crow
|
Graham—Robert—Trevor—Janet

Doris Jaquest's story came through the eyes of one of her sons - Graham Crow. We met at his home in the peaceful surroundings of the Essex countryside. Laid out on the large dining room table were many photographs of the family, including one of his grandfather's restaurant The Sunflower. We talked of his mother's early years and of her life after her marriage to his father Ernest Crow.– CE

Doris Jaquest

Doris Muriel Jaquest was born in 1921, the last of four daughters to be born to Albert and Bessie. Her parents were still running their fruiterers on Eastern Esplanade when her arrival completed the couples family. It would not be until the mid 1930s that her parents opened their restaurant. Like her older siblings Doris attended Brewery Road school, where in 1935 when she was 14 , she won a medal in the Borough sports. This was an annual event that all the local schools participated in. The inscription on the back of her medal reads "relay – 1935- 3rd-D Jaquest". During the school holidays, like her sisters she sometimes helped out in her parents Sunflower restaurant or joined her sisters on the seafront, where they often had picnics.

The Jaquest sisters with their mother Bessie

In the late 1930s attending a dance above the shops in Southchurch Avenue (near where pizza hut stands today 2010) she met her future husband, Ernest Crow. Ernest had been born in West Ham in 1908, but his family had later

Ernest and Doris

moved down to Wickford in Essex. The dance had been organised by the local Co-op Society and provided the young men and women of the town at the time the opportunity to meet and have fun, which all too soon was to come to an end when war was declared. By this time Doris and Ernest had been courting for sometime and after the Jaquests had moved up to North Finchley the couple decided to get married. Doris was the second of the Jaquest girls to get married, during their time away from home. Both Eileen and Doris married within a few months of one another in Hendon in 1940.

When the family returned to Southend-on-Sea within two years, Doris did her bit for the war effort by joining the auxiliary services, by becoming an ambulance driver. Because of its proximity to London and The Thames the area suffered substantial bomb damage. When the war ended the couple were finally able to start their family with Graham arriving first in 1946, to be followed by Robert, Trevor

Ernest and Doris's wedding 1940

and sister Janet. The couple followed the tradition of the Jaquests setting up in business. They opened an ironmongers shop in the London Road, not far from the high street and near where Doris's sisters had their businesses. In those days ironmongers shops were a common sight in shopping areas, a place where you could buy anything from garden tools, buckets, bowls, saucepans and kettles and paraffin for heaters. A little like an Aladdin's cave. The Crow's continued to run their shop for many years before retiring.

Ernest outside his shop

Ernest died 1992 followed by his wife Doris in 1998. Their children still live in the area and one of their son's Graham, followed them into the retail trade.

Patrick Hendry

Leonard & Gladys Jaquest
(nee Walling, no issue)
|
Nephew Patrick Hendry

**Leonard Jaquest holding
Patrick Hendry as a baby**

Patrick Hendry went to live with Leonard and Gladys Jaquest when he was orphaned during the Second World War. Nephew of Gladys he found a welcoming home with the couple who were childless "by the time I came to live with them in the 1940s their businesses on the seafront were already up for sale". When he turned 18 Patrick joined the army and later served in Korea. After his aunt and uncle passed away in the 1970s, part of his legacy was to inherit photos of the couple throughout their life together. As well as old menu cards and photographs of The Beehive restaurant from their time on Eastern Esplanade.

Patrick Hendry

**Patrick Hendry today in his garden
in Maldon**

My thanks to Patrick Hendry, now living in Maldon, for not only sharing his memories of Leonard and Gladys Jaquest but also offering information on some of the staff who worked for them, as well as giving me permission to reproduce some of the family photographs in this book.

Staff Essential

24 THE BEEHIVE 24

Waitresses outside The Beehive

Although the Jaquest family were very much hands on, when it came to running their shops and restaurants, staff were still essential in order that their various business interests ran smoothly. When it came to The Beehive, Star and later The Sunflower restaurant there would have been full and part time staff to help them in the day to day running of their seaside enterprises. An integral part of the service offered by the Jaquests would have been good wholesome food offered at reasonable prices which their neatly turned out waitresses would have served in the light and airy surroundings of their restaurants.

Other staff, just as important to the restaurant business, especially during the main holiday periods, were the young boys and girls, who needed weekend employment or summer jobs during the school holidays. Like young people today, who have paper rounds or work in high street stores at weekends, or at Adventure Island, for extra spending money, the youngsters of the 1930s and 40s were no different, needing work to earn pocket money for themselves or to help with their families finances. These young adults cleared tables, washed up (no dishwashers then) and peeled potatoes.

The following pages reflect just a small number of staff who worked for the Jaquests over many years and their memories and photographs of these times.

The Fruiters Eastern Esplanade

Alfred Frampton
Chef at The Beehive

*Alfred with his wife
Louisa Maria*

George Alfred Frampton was born in West Ham around 1871, his chosen career much later in life to be a cook then a chef could not have been more different from his background. His father Isaac, born in Kent was a stevedore at the Victoria Docks in London and his grandfather George was a policeman.

Cooking was to play an integral part of his whole working life from his humble beginnings as a vegetable cook in a public house, to running his first café with his wife Louisa (nee Rolt) near the Woolwich Docks. Here they served the troops from the First World War their hot mugs of tea, as well as the locals. With quite a large family to support they worked hard with long hours. The decision to move to Essex came soon after the birth of their last child Peggy in 1922. They all moved to the London Road at Leigh-on-Sea where again Alfred and Louisa ran a café serving the locals and any passing trade.

Meeting with his daughter Peggy (now Hart and still living in the area) in 2009 she was unable to tell me why they had given up the business and her father went to work at The Beehive on the seafront. "We moved to a nice house in Brunswick Road, Southend which was quite near the seafront". During the school holidays Peggy would walk to the beehive with her father, staying on to work for Len Jaquest. Her job to wash and prepare the salads for the days trade.

Alfred's specialities were his sultana and his college pudding popular with the towns visitors and the staff of the nearby gas works who would come in to have lunch. By the outbreak of the Second World War Alfred had retired from his job as chef at The Beehive, he continued to live on in the town with his wife until his death when nearly 90 years old.

Mavis Floyd

Mavis Stagg nee Floyd on right of picture

Mavis Floyd was born in Rochford, Essex in 1913. As was the custom in those days working life began at aged 14. Her first job was with Leonard Jaquest as a waitress in The Beehive. Mavis continued working at the restaurant until her marriage in 1936 to Arthur Stagg, who was a serving soldier based at the garrison in Shoeburyness, Essex (now demolished). After the Second World War, Mavis met up again with Leonard and his wife Gladys and became their housekeeper, first in Dowset Avenue then at their bungalow in Thorpe Bay. She continued working for the Jaquests until both had passed away (Gladys in 1974 and Leonard 1975) taking into her care their dog "Micky" who having outlived his owners needed a home. Mavis Stagg continued living in Southend-on-Sea until her death in 1995.

Doris Hallum

Doris Hallum came to The Beehive restaurant around 1933 to work for Leonard and Gladys Jaquest. Just 13 years old she would travel into Southend from Shoeburyness where she lived with her family to work Saturdays and Sundays in the restaurant. Her hours were 8am – 6pm and for this she was paid half a crown. Her job was to peel potatoes and wash up the dishes (no dishwashers then of course). Sometimes Leonard Jaquest would pay Doris an extra 6 pence and she would go round the corner to the Kursaal, pay to ride on the Mat slide which was half a penny and then her final treat would be an ice cream before leaving for home to give her mum her half a crown wages. Today (2009) Doris is nearly 90 and still living locally.

Peggy Hart nee Frampton

Daughter of Alfred Frampton, chef at The Beehive, like Doris, Peggy began working at The Beehive when she was 13 years old, where her job was to wash and prepare the salads. As the family lived quite close to the seafront, Peggy would walk to work with her Dad. Still living in the area with her husband and daughter, Peggy has fond memories of her time working in the restaurant.

Staff Outing
Ivy Harper worked for the Jaquest's as a cashier in the late 1930s
Her daughter June also spent some time there as a waitress.
Ivy is third from the right front row, and daughter June is second from left front row.

Charabanc Excursion
Leonard Jaquest sixth from the right with members of his staff
about to leave for a day out.

Eastern Esplanade

Original Sunflower Restaurant

For the writer or historian researching the history of Eastern Esplanade, Southend-on-Sea there are many sources of information available. From Kelly's Directory, local maps dating back to the 1800s in Southend Library and archive material from Essex Record Office.

Eastern Esplanade note car and horse and cart sharing the road.

Having gleaned a substantial amount of useful material on the subject, I discovered that this strip of land had several different names over the years, before settling for its current title.

At the beginning of the 1800s the majority of the area was more track than a proper road and was known in the very beginning as Southchurch Beach Road. The area during that period was in the very early stages of being developed and different sections carried various names, such as Kursaal Pavement, East Parade and Scott Villas Road. This section was called after one James Scott a successful builder, property speculator and developer and sometime owner of The Royal Hotel, at the top of Pier Hill. In 1858 he sought permission to create a promenade - which would eventually take his name - and would be for the recreation of the inhabitants of the town and its visitors. One of the building conditions stated "that should the promenade be built upon or

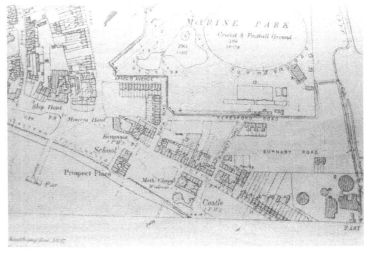

planted with trees or shrubs they must be no higher than four feet". The deeds also named the area he wanted to develop "Fairhead's Green Eastern Esplanade", yet a map dated 1897 still shows Eastern Esplanade as being a beach area opposite Marine Parade, Lower Southend and Scott Villas Road. The company who built Scott Villas the LT and S Lime Company had their work yard nearby. When John Jaquest first put down his roots on the seafront in 1908, his address was Kursaal Pavement, but constant changes occurred over his first few years, no doubt very confusing for the postal service. With some sections of the road in private hands, other sections owned by the council it would be some years before this track would turn into the major seaside road with the name we are familiar with today. This came about in 1913 at a council meeting.

> The committee had under consideration the question of renaming that portion of Esplanade, lying between the Minerva Public House and Thorpe Hall Avenue. In order to abolish the variation of names by which the thoroughfare is at present known, the section between the Minerva and the Half Way House will be called Eastern Esplanade. The road lying east of the Half Way House to be called Thorpe Esplanade.

At last the confusion of the stretch of road with several different names was resolved. Taking the title previously given to the beach opposite Marine Parade, the road became known officially as Eastern Esplanade.

The development of Eastern Esplanade was slightly different to that of Marine Parade which was close by, in that it offered more accommodation for the locals, as well as shops a school - St John's National School and the post office run by Richard and Annie Ashton. Also along this stretch of road was built the Free Methodist Chapel, its trustees were the local blacksmith and carpenter. By the late 1890s the Southend Gas Company would hold a prominent position opposite the Thames, on Eastern Esplanade complete with a governor's house and offices. The company was started in 1854 when a Mr W Warwick called a meeting with a view to forming a company that would provide the area with lighting and heat. Among its first directors was a Vandervord (local wealthy barge owning family) finding the land to open the first depot was made easy when the Lord of the Manor, Daniel Scratton, donated a four acre site on his land at Prittlewell.

Further along the road the address given, as Southchurch Beach Road stood "The Cripples Home" (a term that would not be used today) which was run by the Shaftesbury and Ragged School Union, whose patron was Lord Shaftesbury. The home was still offering places to these unfortunate children as late as 1917. The growth of the area did not neglect the traveller, nor the locals in need of a good beer, along its path was The Army and Navy Public House, Castle Hotel and The Halfway House.

Along the way in flats houses or fisherman's cottages were a mixture of people from all walks of life, living in close proximity to one another. Henry Smith, manager of the Southchurch Brickfields, which stretched between Shoeburyness and Southend - the brickfields were owned by the Welch family. In 1891 they leased the business to a James Helby of Herne Bay who was a retired Admiralty clerk. Further along the road was a lodging house, its landlady one Louisa Webster, a widow, who was born and bred in Camberwell. Standing close by was The

To the left the original Sunflower Restaurant demolished early 1900s. To the right the Free Methodist Chapel demolished 1930s

Britannia public house which was near the Kursaal, its address given as East Parade. The Britannia still stands in the same spot today. In 1901 Charles Absalom, fisherman and Robert Thorby a butcher had taken up residence along Eastern Esplanade as well as a Ralph Deglow a hairdresser, who had lived with his family in Cable Street London before moving to Southend, where he continued his trade. His family originally came from Berlin. At number 3 East Parade was Herbert Sawkins with his coffee shop - The Star (later the fish shop of John Jaquest and in the 1930s taken over by Leonard Jaquest who took it back to its original use and name). The clergy were represented by Edward Thounton a Church of England minster, who lived with his mother a school mistress. Watermen and master mariners naturally formed a greater part of the

The Beehive Restaurant in its heyday

population on this road, which was so close to the River Thames, but they shared this space with a milkman and one William Emms who was a portrait painter originally from Shoreditch. For many others the only occupations available to them were common labouring or being in service as a way of making their living and paying their rent for the various abodes spread along Eastern Esplanade

Today the area nearest the amusement arcades has seen some re-generation as following the Second World War it became quite a run down part of Southend. There is the fish and chip shop, pubs and other food outlets and the original fisherman's cottages still remain, in remarkably good condition.

In 1926 the Beehive Restaurant which was vacant—was advertised for sale by Talbot and White of Clarence Street. The property was owned at that time by the Hopkinson family. The auctioneers describe the premises as:

"Most successfully carried on as a restaurant. The property occupies unquestionably one of the busiest positions on the seafront, which is phenomenal for its extensive trading."

Further details revealed that at the rear of the restaurant was a brick built building, with four living rooms. Plus a covered yard with seating for sixty people and a WC. The kitchen was described as having a large range and dresser. The only information not provided by the auctioneers was the asking price for this going concern.

Some of the buildings occupied by the Jaquests have been modernised at street level, it is only if the passerby cares to look up will they see a plaster moulding in the shape of a Beehive above the second floor windows of 24 Eastern Esplanade where the Beehive restaurant stood until 1946.

24 Eastern Esplanade, 2010.

The Jaquest Legacy

When I began working on this book, having been introduced to Queenie Ife nee Jaquest, by her granddaughter Wendy Clarke, I saw only the history of the family's restaurants and shops, that had stood on Eastern Esplanade between 1908 – 1947. I wrongly concluded that having been an integral part of the seaside trade for nearly forty years that the sale of The Beehive and Sunflower restaurants brought to a close the family's association with the catering and retail trade in the town, that had begun with John and Emily Jaquest. They were followed by two of their sons, Albert and Leonard who sold their businesses (restaurants) that were situated on Eastern Esplanade after the Second World War. I thought this was where the family's story might have end but it was to continue with Albert and Bessie Jaquest's children and grandchildren for the next sixty years.

When reading many of the books written about southend, in particular the High Street, the names often quoted are Garons, Keddies, Ravens and R A Jones. All these family run establishments held prominent positions in the main shopping area for many years. Although the Jaquest's daughters and their husbands never had a business in the High Street they remained a strong influence around the town with their various enterprises which included an ironmongers, the café in Priory Park – still serving food and drink today - a coffee bar, to cater for the latest teenage craze in the 1960s, a DIY shop and another café in the London Road, Southend. It would fall to one of the grandsons – Graham Crow, to have the only business to stand on Southend High Street.

Son of Doris (Jaquest) and Ernest Crow his working life began at 16 as an apprentice bricklayer for C W Pavey. A long established firm of builders in Southend their workshop was sited at 196 Hamlet Court Road, however, when Graham joined the firm in October 1961 only the original name remained, as the builders had been bought out by a Frank Hughes. Three years later in 1966 he left Paveys to buy his uncle's DIY shop, in the Victoria Arcade, which led into the more well known part of the complex The Talza Arcade, near Victoria Circus. Built in 1926 the lanes were made up of a row of small shops, offering a diversity of goods, such as shoes, clothes, books and pets for sale. The Arcade was demolished in the late 1960s to make way for a modern shopping complex and it was to here that Graham Crow moved his DIY business in 1968, but just two

Graham Crow (centre) in front of his DIY shop

years later he changed direction completely and opened the first of his eight newsagents in Cliff Town Road. Next came a position in the old bus station in the London Road (now Sainsbury's) this was followed in 1974, by a franchise in Keddies department store. Two years later a Crow's newsagents was occupying a prominent position of its own on the High Street, standing where today (2010) you will find the book chain Waterstone's. Between 1988 – 1994 four more shops would be opened around the town. Bournemouth Park Road, on Victoria Railway Station – Alexander Street and Southchurch. Graham Crow continued running his chain of newsagents until 2007 when he sold his eight shops and took early retirement.

Queenie and Howard behind the bar of the Chalkwell Park Rooms 1975

Another of the grandson's, Howard Ife, son of Queenie (Jaquest) and Frederick Ife was determined not to follow his parents into the catering business. Instead he became an electrician and worked in the building industry for a few years. In 1973 an advertisement in the local paper offered for sale the café that stood in Chalkwell Park. The building at that time was owned by Southend Council. The park which stands by the busy London Road at Westcliff-on-Sea has always been a popular place for families to visit. In the summer months cricket was, and still is, played on the large pitch directly opposite to where the Chalkwell Park Rooms stood, but today (2010), the venue is called Park View Suite. Unable to talk Howard out of buying the café, telling him of the long hours and hard work that would be needed to make the business a success, Queenie went into partnership with her son. The café was well placed to serve refreshments, light snacks and ice creams from April until October. In 1975 Howard felt his business had more potential if extensive alterations were made to the building and permission given to open all year round including evenings for private functions. He applied to the council for permission to extend and develop the site, although initially there were some objections, permission was finally granted.

Chalkwell Park Rooms

invite you to hold your ★ DINNER DANCES ★ BUFFET SUPPERS ★ BUSINESS LUNCHES ★ WEDDING RECEPTIONS ★ PRIVATE PARTIES ★ WEDDING RECEPTIONS ★ WINE AND CHEESE SOCIALS In the delightful surroundings of Chalkwell Park. We can offer excellent food at competitive prices, all arranged under the personal supervision of Howard Ife.

LICENSED BAR   MIDDAY LUNCHES SERVED   **Tel: Southend 7 9 1 6 2**

Photograph taken in 1980

During the day the venue was open to the general public offering traditional English lunches, following in the footsteps of his grandfather Albert Jaquest, who in the 1930s and 40s had offered much the same type of food, from his restaurant on Eastern Esplanade. The new venture was an immediate success and as well as offering lunches, the venue proved popular for wedding receptions and other special occasions. In the evening, groups and associations would use the venue for their annual dinner dances and meetings. In 1976 The Jurade Des Maitres Queux De Belique held their "Belge Banquet and Ball" in the Chalkwell Rooms. Slightly more controversial the Southend East Conservative Association (Southchurch Ward) had booked the Rt. Hon. Enoch Powell as their guest speaker for their annual dinner on

SOUTHEND EAST CONSERVATIVE ASSOCIATION

SOUTHCHURCH WARD

The Chairman and Committee
welcome you to a

B A N Q U E T

to be held at

CHALKWELL PARK BANQUETING SUITE

on

FRIDAY, 24th APRIL, 1981

Guest Speaker
The Rt. Hon. ENOCH POWELL, M.P.

Reception 7.15 - 7.45 p.m.   *Tickets £9.50*   *Dress - Lounge Suit*
THIS CARD MUST BE PRODUCED ON ADMISSION

Friday 24th April 1981. With his outspoken attitude to immigration, his arrival that night at Chalkwell Park was greeted by a large crowd of hecklers, who had to be kept back by the police. Once the MP was inside the building, the rest of the evening passed without incident.

The venue's popularity was such that within a few years Howard Ife and his wife took over The New Arlington Rooms that stood close by, just the other side of the main road, to cope with the bookings. One advantage of The Arlington Rooms was that it offered much more floor space and the couple branched out into advertising the premises as suitable for trade fairs and exhibitions.

Luncheon

In the presence of

HRH the Princess Anne

Friday 2nd May 1986

As well as organising the usual dinner dances, parties and meetings, Howard secured the contract with Southend Council to cater for the many civic occasions that took place in the town. One rather special event was when Princess Anne came to the town in 1986, to launch the new RNLI lifeboat and to see the latest pier trains go into service. Later that day there was a civic reception for the royal guest, the mayor and local dignitaries at Porters* with Howard Ife responsible for the catering.

In 1989 Howard and his wife gave up running the Chalkwell Park Rooms to concentrate on their other venue The New Arlington, but by 1995 the couple had sold this business as well. Howard Ife returned to the building industry, following yet another family tradition set by his great grandfather - John Jaquest – who had started his working life with bricks and mortar, before entering the world of catering. With his family, like his cousin Graham Crow, Howard still lives locally.

*(this is a late 15th century Grade I listed building, the official residence of the Mayor and Mayoress of Southend-on-Sea)

The Jaquest's of Southend-on-Sea and their descendants have proved themselves to be a versatile and hardworking family through four generations, two world wars, constant changing social patterns and have adapted to them all.

Leonard Jaquest
1899—1975

John Jaquest
1854—1939

Albert Jaquest
1884—1983

The daughters of Albert and Bessie Jaquest who through their marriages and children would continue the Jaquest story.

Carol Edwards was born in Hendon but moved to Westcliff-on-Sea with her family in 1947. She was educated at Westborough School, MacDonald Avenue, Westcliff. Working for Customs and Excise for 25 years during which time as a member of their Sports and Social Club she was also Editor of their in-house magazine "Touchline". A freelance writer for the past few years her work has mainly appeared in magazines and local newspapers Seaside Entrepreneurs is her second local history book. Her first was the "Life and Times of the Houseboats of Leigh"..

She is married with two daughters and three grandchildren.